Personal Wellness Rx: Your Daily Self-Care Vitamins for
Mindfulness and Emotional Wellness

Dr. LaQuenta Long, PsyD, LMFT

Welcome to "Personal Wellness Rx." I'm excited to have you join me on this path to better well-being and a balanced life. This book is more than just about talking self-care; it's here to help you create a self-care plan that supports your mental health in a complete way.

I know your daily schedule can be busy, but taking time for your body, mind, and emotions can make a big difference. Just like vitamins are key to physical health, self-care activities are essential for mental and emotional strength. As you read the chapters ahead, you'll learn personalized strategies to tailor your self-care to what your mind and emotions really need.

We all know we should do more self-care or make it a regular habit. I hope that by viewing self-care as a vitamin supplement, you broaden your approach and create a plan that revives and supports you mentally and emotionally on your wellness journey.

Thank you for letting this guide be part of your journey. Here's to your health, happiness, and harmony.

Dr. Laquenta Long

TABLE OF CONTENTS

Discover how
Self-Care Vitamins
can transform
your daily life,

"The journey
of thousand
miles miles
begins with
a single step,"
— Lao Tzu

Introduction

Welcome to "Personal Wellness Rx," your helpful guide to creating a wellness plan that goes beyond simple self-care activities. Just like your body needs different things to stay healthy, your mind needs variety too. Taking care of your body means many things—keeping your heart strong, your stomach happy, and your bones healthy. This book shows you how to use that same idea for your mind and emotions.

Think about how vitamins help your body. Vitamin C protects you from getting sick. Vitamin D keeps your bones strong. Without enough vitamins, you can have problems like weak bones or getting sick more often. Your mind works the same way. It needs different types of self-care to stay strong and handle stress.

Our world moves fast. We face pressure from school, work, family, and friends every day. When we don't manage this stress well, we can feel overwhelmed or sad. That's where self-care comes in. It's like giving your mind the vitamins it needs to stay calm and happy.

Different self-care activities help in different ways. Mindfulness and meditation bring peace and help you focus. Exercise releases special chemicals that make you feel good and give you energy. Time with friends and family provides support when you need it. These activities are mental health vitamins. They make you stronger and more balanced, so daily challenges become easier.

Without self-care, things can get tough. You might feel more stressed and tired. Simple tasks stop being fun. You could feel lonely and disconnected. But when you make time for self-care, you can prevent these problems and feel much better.

This book helps you discover which self-care activities work best for you. You'll learn how to stay aware, find balance, and stay connected to others. You'll see why exercise matters and how to clear negative thoughts from your mind. With the right self-care plan, handling stress becomes easier.

"Personal Wellness Rx" shows you how to balance your body, mind, and emotions. This balance creates a happier, healthier life. Use this guide to become stronger on the inside. Soon, your mind, body, and emotions will work together like a well-tuned team.

Book Structure Overview

In the chapters ahead, you'll explore five essential self-care vitamins that support your mental and emotional health. Vitamin A for Awareness helps you understand your thoughts and feelings better. Vitamin B for Balance shows you how to manage your time and energy across all areas of life. Vitamin C for Connection guides you in building meaningful relationships. Vitamin D for Detox teaches you to clear away negative thoughts and experiences. Finally, Vitamin E for Exercise demonstrates how physical activity boosts your mental health. Each vitamin chapter includes signs of deficiency and practical activities to strengthen that area of your life.

How to Use This Book

This book is designed to fit your unique needs and schedule. You can read it from beginning to end to get a complete understanding of all five self-care vitamins. Or, if you're facing a specific challenge, jump directly to the chapter that addresses your current needs. Each section includes simple self-assessment questions to help you identify areas that need attention. You'll also find easy activities you can start today. Take your time with each chapter. Try the suggested activities and see what works best for you. Remember, building a self-care routine is a personal journey, not a race.

What Makes This Book Different

Many self-care books can feel overwhelming with long lists of things to do. This guide is different because it uses something you already understand—vitamins. Just like you know your body needs Vitamin C when you're getting sick, this book helps you recognize when your mind needs specific types of care. The vitamin approach makes self-care simple and memorable. Instead of trying to do everything at once, you can focus on the specific "vitamin" you need most right now. This method transforms confusing wellness advice into clear, actionable steps anyone can follow.

Personal Connection

This vitamin approach to self-care isn't just theory—it's been tested in real life. Through my own journey and working with many others, I've seen how viewing self-care as vitamins changes everything. People who once felt overwhelmed by self-care advice suddenly understood exactly what they needed. A busy parent realized she was low on Vitamin C (Connection) and started scheduling weekly coffee dates with friends. A stressed student discovered his Vitamin B (Balance) deficiency and began setting boundaries with his study time. These simple shifts, guided by the vitamin framework, led to real improvements in their daily lives and overall happiness.

Interactive Elements

Throughout this book, you'll find helpful tools to make your self-care journey personal and practical. Each chapter includes reflection questions to help you think about your current habits and needs. You'll discover checklists to track your progress and blank spaces to write your thoughts and plans. At the end of each vitamin section, there's room to create your own self-care activities based on what you've learned. The final chapter brings everything together, helping you build a complete self-care plan that fits your life. These interactive parts turn this book from something you just read into something you actively use to improve your well-being.

Knowledge is the foundation of self-care"

Learn the powerful connection
between vitamins and self-care

1 Understanding the Vitamin Metaphor

Sometimes your self-care activities don't seem to help much. You might want to stop doing them and focus on other tasks that feel more productive. But these "productive" tasks can drain your energy if they don't support your overall health and happiness. Real self-care means understanding exactly what you need. It's not just about taking breaks—it's about doing activities that help your mind, body, and emotions stay strong.

The Vitamin Approach to Self-Care

Self-care works just like vitamins for your body. Different vitamins do different jobs, and you need to take them regularly to stay healthy. You don't wait until you're sick to start taking vitamins. The same goes for self-care. It works best when you do it every day, not just when you're having a crisis. Regular self-care keeps your mind and emotions healthy, just like vitamins keep your body healthy.

A Simple Example: Vitamin D

Let's look at Vitamin D. It keeps your bones strong by helping your body use calcium. You need to take it regularly to prevent bone problems. Once your bones get weak, vitamins can't fix the damage—they can only stop it from getting worse. Self-care works the same way. Activities like relaxation, spending time with friends, or exercising keep your mind and emotions strong. Don't wait until you're stressed or upset to start. Regular self-care prevents problems before they happen.

Three Keys to Effective Self-Care

To make self-care work like vitamins, remember these three things:

1. Know what area needs help. Do you need better focus? More energy? Stronger friendships? Pick the right "vitamin" for your specific need.
2. Check your current condition. Are you slightly tired or completely exhausted? Knowing where you stand helps you choose the right response.
3. Figure out the right dose. Some activities work best daily, others weekly. Finding the right frequency makes all the difference.

Without thinking about these three things, you might pick activities that don't really help. It's like taking the wrong vitamin or not taking enough to make a difference.

Choosing the Right Wellness Zone

When someone tells you to practice self-care, you might think about relaxing or treating yourself. These are good ideas, but they're too vague. To really help yourself, you need to be specific about what you need.
Start by asking yourself questions. How does your body feel? If you're tired, do you need rest or do you need to build strength? Rest might mean taking a nap or meditating. Building strength might mean exercising. The right choice depends on your specific situation.

Think ahead too. What challenges are coming up? If you're starting something new, self-care might mean gathering information or finding people who can help. If you love reading, pick books that address your current needs. This makes your self-care time more valuable.

Getting Help from Others

Sometimes we miss what we really need because we're too focused on daily tasks. That's when friends and family can help. They might notice changes we don't see in ourselves.

Ask people close to you what they've noticed. Have you stopped doing things you used to enjoy? Has your mood changed? Are there goals you talked about but haven't pursued? Their observations can guide your self-care choices.

Think of this like choosing add-ons at a smoothie shop. The shop offers different boosters—energy, protein, immunity. If you know what you need, you can pick the right one. If you don't know, you might skip it or or choose randomly. Self-care works the same way. Knowing what you need helps you make better choices.

Understanding Your Wellness Levels

Your mind, body, and emotions tell you where you are on your wellness journey. Pay attention to all three. Ask yourself: Are things going well, or do I see warning signs? This helps you know whether to maintain what you're doing or make changes.

Look at specific areas. How do you handle feedback from others? Do you get defensive or use it to improve? Can you manage stress without snapping at people? These reactions show how well you're managing your emotions.

Your body gives clues too. Have your sleep patterns changed? What about your appetite? Do you get more headaches than usual? Physical symptoms often reflect emotional stress. Paying attention helps you catch problems early.

Listen to feedback from others, even when it's hard to hear. Know the difference between helpful observations and harmful criticism. When someone who cares about you notices changes, take it seriously. They're not trying to hurt you—they're helping you see what you might be missing.

Getting the Right Amount of Self-Care

A self-care routine only works when you do it at the right frequency. Think about vacations. You feel great afterward, but the feeling fades quickly when you return to normal life. This happens because vacations alone aren't enough. You need regular self-care at different intervals.

Daily self-care keeps you going each day. This includes basics like:

- Getting enough sleep
- Eating healthy meals
- Taking short breaks
- Doing brief exercises

Weekly self-care helps you recharge for the week ahead. Try:

- Spending quality time with friends or family
- Doing a hobby you enjoy
- Taking care of personal needs like haircuts
- Having a longer exercise session

Monthly self-care rewards you for making it through the month. Consider:

- Getting a massage
- Buying something special you've saved for
- Attending a workshop or class
- Taking a day trip somewhere peaceful

Yearly self-care gives you bigger goals to work toward. Plan for:

- Vacations or retreats
- Major purchases that support your well-being
- Big experiences you've dreamed about
- Annual health check-ups

This variety keeps self-care interesting and effective. If you only think of self-care as big vacations, it seems impossible to maintain. But when you include daily and weekly activities, it becomes a natural part of life. You'll feel better every day, not just during rare breaks from routine.

Nourishing yourself in a way that helps you blossom in the direction you want to go is attainable, and you are worth the effort.
Deborah Day

Awareness is like the sun.
When it shines on things,
they are transformed.

Discover the power of
mindfulness and self-awareness

2 Self-Care Vitamin A - Awareness

Self-care Vitamin A is all about awareness—understanding yourself better. This means taking time to think about who you are and how you feel. Often, we get so busy with daily tasks like homework, chores, or work that we forget to pay attention to ourselves. We focus on getting things done instead of checking in with our own thoughts and feelings.

Why Awareness Matters

Self-awareness helps you understand your thoughts, feelings, and actions. When you know yourself better, you can spot what makes you stressed or upset before it becomes a big problem. Instead of reacting without thinking, you can pause and choose how to respond. This helps you build better friendships, reach your goals, and make choices that match what's really important to you.

Mindfulness goes hand-in-hand with self-awareness. It means paying attention to what's happening right now without worrying about yesterday or tomorrow. When you practice mindfulness, you worry less and enjoy life more. It also helps you handle tough times better. Together, self-awareness and mindfulness make life more balanced and satisfying.

Signs You Need More Vitamin A

Here are some signs that you might need to work on your awareness. Remember, you don't need all these signs to benefit from building awareness. Use this list to think about whether you need more self-care in this area.

Take care of your body. It's the only place you have to live.
Jim Rohn

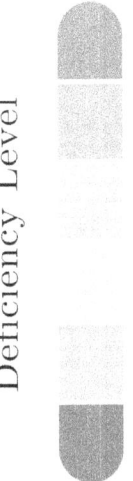

Deficiency Level

Impulsive Reaction

This means responding without thinking about how it might affect others or considering their feelings. You might react this way because there's something you need that isn't being met. You may know what you need, or it might be something you've overlooked. Your quick reaction is a clue that you're missing something important.

What would this look like for you? :

_____

_____

_____

Consider the reason why this would be a deficiency for you?

_____

_____

_____

What are the supportive reason improve this self care supplement?

_____

_____

_____

Deficiency Level

Difficulty Identifying Emotions

Sometimes, it's hard to understand your own feelings. People might ask if something's wrong because they notice a change, but you might not realize it or figure out what's bothering you.

What would this look like for you? :

_____

_____

_____

Consider the reason why this would be a deficiency for you?

_____

_____

_____

What are the supportive reason improve this self care supplement?

_____

_____

_____

Lack of Insight

You might not notice how your actions affect others. For example, you could be busy with your daily tasks and not realize your family misses spending time with you. What you're doing is important, but you might not see how it makes your family feel.

Deficiency Level

What would this look like for you? :

_____

_____

_____

Consider the reason why this would be a deficiency for you?

_____

_____

_____

What are the supportive reason improve this self care supplement?

_____

_____

_____

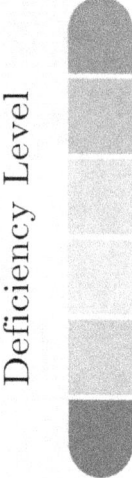

Deficiency Level

Poor Decision Making

Sometimes, you might make a decision that doesn't match your values or what's best for you. For example, you might say yes to something without thinking about how it will affect other parts of your life. Or you might ignore an opportunity and regret it later. These choices often happen because you react quickly instead of taking time to be reflective.

What would this look like for you? :

_____

_____

Consider the reason why this would be a deficiency for you?

_____

_____

What are the supportive reason improve this self care supplement?

_____

_____

Blaming Others

In this situation, you might focus on what others aren't doing and forget to think about your role in things. For example, you might often comment on what someone isn't doing at home or work without realizing you never told them you needed help. Or, you might feel you're not spending enough time with your partner, but maybe your schedule has changed. You notice they're not around, but forget to look at what you can do to change that.

Deficiency Level

What would this look like for you? :

_____

_____

_____

Consider the reason why this would be a deficiency for you?

_____

_____

_____

What are the supportive reason improve this self care supplement?

_____

_____

_____

Inconsistent Behavior

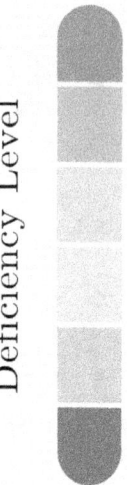

Deficiency Level

Sometimes, your actions might not match how you usually behave, making them seem unpredictable. For example, you could be very supportive and interested in something one moment, and then suddenly, you're dismissive and uninterested for no apparent reason.

What would this look like for you? :

_____

_____

Consider the reason why this would be a deficiency for you?

_____

_____

What are the supportive reason improve this self care supplement?

_____

_____

Denial of Personal Issues

In this situation, you might not realize there's something you need to improve about yourself. You might notice it but choose to ignore it, or you may have been doing it for so long that it feels normal and doesn't seem like a problem to you.

Deficiency Level

What would this look like for you? :

_____

_____

_____

Consider the reason why this would be a deficiency for you?

_____

_____

_____

What are the supportive reason improve this self care supplement?

_____

_____

_____

The signs listed here to help you think about your own experiences. You don't need to have all of these signs—maybe none fit, but you notice something else about yourself. This is all about being aware. Reflect on what you need and what's happening with you. Be mindful of how you go through your day and whether it matches with taking care of yourself.

Knowing yourself is the beginning of all wisdom. Aristotle

Vitamin A Supplemental Activities

Now that you recognize the signs of low awareness, it's time to build up your Vitamin A levels. These activities are like exercises for your mind—they help you tune in to your thoughts, feelings, and body signals. Just like learning any new skill, building awareness takes practice. Some activities might feel strange at first, and that's normal. The good news is you don't need special equipment or lots of time. Even a few minutes of practice can make a difference. Start with activities that appeal to you most, and remember there's no "perfect" way to do them. The goal is simply to become more connected with yourself. Let's explore different ways to strengthen your self-awareness and mindfulness.

Meditation:

A meditation routine is about finding a place where you can focus on your breathing and clear your mind. This helps you notice your thoughts and feelings right now. There are traditional ways to meditate, but you can also fit meditation into your everyday life in other simple ways.

Morning Meditation

Find a quiet spot in your home, maybe early in the morning before everyone else wakes up, and spend 5-10 minutes focusing on your breath. You can also think about what you want to achieve that day and how you plan to handle whatever comes your way.

Frequency you look to participate in this activity:

Daily ·········· Weekly ··········· Monthly ··········· Yearly

Time allotted to spend for this activity:

What what ways will this activity support your mental well-being?

_____

_____

_____

_____

Create a value statement for what you are looking to gain by participating in this activity?

66

99

During your lunch break, take a few minutes to meditate. Find a quiet place, either inside or outside, and spend that time clearing your mind and relaxing.

Lunchtime Reset

Frequency you look to participate in this activity:

Daily ·········· Weekly ·········· Monthly ·········· Yearly

Time allotted to spend for this activity:

What what ways will this activity support your mental well-being?

_____

_____

_____

_____

Create a value statement for what you are looking to gain by participating in this activity?

66

Break-time Mindfulness

Find times in your day to focus on your mind and body. Take a moment to check in purposely and see how you're feeling.

Frequency you look to participate in this activity:

Daily ·········· Weekly ·········· Monthly ·········· Yearly

Time allotted to spend for this activity:

What what ways will this activity support your mental well-being?

_____

_____

_____

_____

Create a value statement for what you are looking to gain by participating in this activity?

66 _____ 99

Make a transition time between different parts of your day, like when you finish work and start your time at home. Use this time to let go of work stress and focus on being present at home.

End of the Day Wind Down

Frequency you look to participate in this activity:

Daily ·········· Weekly ··········· Monthly ··········· Yearly

Time allotted to spend for this activity:

What what ways will this activity support your mental well-being?

_____

_____

_____

_____

Create a value statement for what you are looking to gain by participating in this activity?

66

99

Making time for meditation is simple. It's about paying attention to what's happening in your mind, body, and feelings. This helps you notice slight changes before they become bigger problems. By recognizing these shifts, you can make changes in your life to prevent unwanted thoughts and moods later on.

Journaling:

There are many ways to journal, and lots of resources can help you with it. Journaling is a time to think about yourself. It's not about judging yourself, but about noticing what's happening. When you understand your thoughts better, you can see how you handle life's challenges. Journaling also gives you a chance to change and grow.

**Awareness is like the sun.
When it shines on things,
they are transformed.
Thich Nhat Hanh**

Intentions Journal

This kind of journaling is about thinking ahead about how you want to act in different situations. It's taking time to figure out how you want to be there for yourself or others. You can do this type of journaling daily, weekly, or whenever you have a moment. The goal is to be clear on your intentions before you need to act.

Frequency you look to participate in this activity:

Daily ·········· Weekly ·········· Monthly ·········· Yearly

Time allotted to spend for this activity:

What what ways will this activity support your mental well-being?

_____

_____

_____

_____

Create a value statement for what you are looking to gain by participating in this activity?

66

99

A gratitude journal helps you notice the good things in your life. You can write about how you handled a tough situation, the small acts of kindness from others, or the big things you've achieved. Focusing on the positive gives you a strong foundation to handle challenges.

Gratitude Journal

Frequency you look to participate in this activity:

Daily ·········· Weekly ··········· Monthly ··········· Yearly

Time allotted to spend for this activity:

What what ways will this activity support your mental well-being?

_____

_____

_____

_____

Create a value statement for what you are looking to gain by participating in this activity?

❝ _____

_____ ❞

Prompted Journal

This type of journal uses guided questions to help you think. If there's an area in your life you want to understand better, a prompted journal can help. It encourages you to think about things you might not have noticed before, making you more aware of your thoughts, actions, and experiences.

Frequency you look to participate in this activity:

Daily ·········· Weekly ·········· Monthly ·········· Yearly

Time allotted to spend for this activity:

What what ways will this activity support your mental well-being?

_____

_____

_____

_____

Create a value statement for what you are looking to gain by participating in this activity?

66

99

This journal is for writing quick thoughts about your day's experiences. Days are often full of activities and emotions, making it hard to remember details. You might just call a day "long" or "busy." A highlight journal helps you notice what specific events affected your mood or how much you accomplished.

Daily Highlights Journal

Frequency you look to participate in this activity:

Daily ········· Weekly ·········· Monthly ·········· Yearly

Time allotted to spend for this activity:

What what ways will this activity support your mental well-being?

_____

_____

_____

_____

Create a value statement for what you are looking to gain by participating in this activity?

66

99

Body Scan:

  This self-care activity helps you pay attention to what your body feels. Noticing changes in your body can improve your wellness. Even if you're not thinking about stress, knowing how your body reacts can remind you to take breaks when needed. A body scan involves checking each part of your body one at a time. As you become more aware of your body, you'll be able to deal with stress or discomfort more quickly.

Be mindful.
Be grateful.
Be positive.
Be true.
Be kind.
Roy T. Bennett

Progressive Muscle Relaxation

This activity helps you notice where you feel tension in your body and how to let it go. You focus on one area at a time. First, tighten your muscles, hold for a few seconds, and then slowly relax them. Doing this teaches you where you store tension, becoming a signal to pay attention to stress. We often miss subtle signs like tight muscles, which can be early warnings that stress is affecting our body in unhealthy ways.

Frequency you look to participate in this activity:

Daily ·········· Weekly ··········· Monthly ··········· Yearly

Time allotted to spend for this activity:

What what ways will this activity support your mental well-being?

_____

_____

_____

_____

Create a value statement for what you are looking to gain by participating in this activity?

66

99

Stretching is a simple activity that can have lasting benefits. While you stretch, take time to notice how your body reacts. Pay attention to which parts feel good with gentle movements and which one's need more time to loosen up. Regular stretching not only helps relax your muscles but also helps you notice how your body feels after a long day or before doing other activities.

Mindful Stretching

Frequency you look to participate in this activity:

Daily ·········· Weekly ············ Monthly ············ Yearly

Time allotted to spend for this activity:

What what ways will this activity support your mental well-being?

_____

_____

_____

_____

Create a value statement for what you are looking to gain by participating in this activity?

66

99

Breath Focus

Paying attention to your breathing can really help you notice changes in yourself. Find a quiet place without many distractions and close your eyes. Focus on how your breath feels as you breathe in and out. By doing this, you can learn about your breathing pattern and notice how it changes depending on what's going on around you.

Frequency you look to participate in this activity:

Daily ·········· Weekly ··········· Monthly ··········· Yearly

Time allotted to spend for this activity:

What what ways will this activity support your mental well-being?

_____

_____

_____

_____

Create a value statement for what you are looking to gain by participating in this activity?

66

Building awareness doesn't require huge changes. Start with one activity that appeals to you. Maybe it's two minutes of morning breathing or writing three things you're grateful for before bed. Small, consistent practices build big results over time.

As you develop awareness, you'll notice patterns in your thoughts, feelings, and behaviors. You'll catch stress earlier and respond more thoughtfully to challenges. Most importantly, you'll understand yourself better—and that's the foundation for a happier, healthier life.

The first step toward change is awareness. The second step is acceptance. Nathaniel Branden

S E L F   C A R E   V I T A M I N   A

D e f e c i e n c y   A s s e s s m e n t

Instructions: For each statement, check the number that best describes how often this is true for you.

Rating Scale:

1 = Never/Rarely 2 = Sometimes 3 = Often 4 = Always/Almost Always

---

PART 1: Emotional Awareness	1	2	3	4
1. I can identify and name my emotions when I'm feeling them.				
2. I notice physical sensations (like tension or butterflies) that signal different emotions.				
3. I understand why I'm feeling a certain way, not just what I'm feeling.				
4. I can tell the difference between similar emotions (like frustrated vs. angry, or nervous vs. excited).				
5. When my mood changes, I notice it happening.				

Part 1   Score: ___/20

PART 2: Mindful Prescence	1	2	3	4
6. I catch myself when my mind wanders during conversations.				
7. I notice details in my environment (sounds, sights, smells) throughout the day.				
8. I eat meals without distractions like TV or phone.				
9. I take moments to pause and breathe during busy days.				
10. I'm aware of my thoughts without getting completely lost in them.				

Part 2   Score: ___/20

PART 3: Behavioral Awareness	1	2	3	4
11. I think before reacting to situations.				
12. I notice my habits and patterns (both good and bad).				
13. I recognize when I'm about to make a decision I might regret.				
14. I understand how my actions affect others.				
15. I catch myself before saying something hurtful or impulsive.				

Part 3   Score: ___/20

PART 4: Body Awareness	1	2	3	4
16. I notice when I'm holding tension in my body.				
17. I recognize my body's signals for hunger, tiredness, and stress.				
18. I'm aware of my breathing throughout the day.				
19. I notice how different foods or activities make my body feel.				
20. I can sense when I'm getting sick or run down before it gets bad				

Part 4   Score: ___/20

PART 5: Self-Reflection	1	2	3	4
21. I regularly think about my goals and values.				
22. I learn from my mistakes rather than just feeling bad about them.				
23. I question my assumptions and consider different perspectives.				
24. I set aside time to reflect on my day or week.				
25. I'm honest with myself about my strengths and areas for growth.				

Part 5   Score: ___/20

Calculate Your Total Vitamin A Level:

Add all five part scores: _____/100

Understanding Your Results:

Total Score 80-100: High Awareness - Vitamin A Strong!

You have excellent self-awareness! You're tuned in to your thoughts, feelings, and body. Keep maintaining these awareness practices. Consider teaching others or trying advanced mindfulness techniques.

Your focus: Maintain your practices and help others develop awareness.

Total Score 60-79: Moderate Awareness - Vitamin A Good

You have solid awareness in many areas with room for growth. You catch yourself sometimes but miss things at other times. This is a great foundation to build on!

Your focus: Strengthen weak areas and be more consistent with awareness practices.

Total Score 40-59: Developing Awareness - Vitamin A Needs Boost

You're beginning to develop awareness but often run on autopilot. You might feel like life is happening TO you rather than being an active participant. Time to increase your Vitamin A intake!

Your focus: Start with one simple awareness practice daily, like a 5-minute body scan.

Total Score Under 40: Low Awareness - Vitamin A Deficiency

You're often disconnected from your inner experience, which can lead to impulsive decisions and emotional overwhelm. Don't worry—awareness is a skill anyone can develop!

Your focus: Begin with basic practices like noting three emotions daily or taking three conscious breaths.

Your Vitamin A Prescription:

Based on your total score, choose your awareness-building plan:

Score 80-100: Continue current practices + try one new advanced technique monthly

Score 60-79: 10 minutes daily awareness practice + weekly reflection session

Score 40-59: 5 minutes morning awareness + 5 minutes evening reflection

Score Under 40: Start with 3 minutes daily of any awareness practice

Quick Start Activities:

Choose ONE to start today:

☐ Set three "awareness alarms" on your phone for emotion check-ins

☐ Write down three things you noticed about yourself today

☐ Take five mindful breaths right now

☐ Do a 2-minute body scan from head to toe

☐ Journal for 5 minutes about how you're feeling

Remember: Building awareness is like strengthening a muscle. Start small, be patient, and celebrate every bit of progress. Even noticing that you're NOT aware is a form of awareness!

My Vitamin A Goal for This Week:

Date: Initial Score:

Balance is
not something you find,
it's something you create.

Master the art of
life Balance

3 Self-Care Vitamin B - Balance

Finding balance in life is something many people struggle with. When we count the hours in our day, work usually takes up more time than anything else. But real balance isn't just about counting hours—it's about something much deeper.

What Balance Really Means

Balance in your mental and emotional health means paying attention to how much energy you use each day and making sure you restore what you've spent. Every part of your life—work, school, family, and friends—needs your thoughts, emotions, and physical energy. Problems start when we give too much without getting anything back.

Think about eating. We need food to live, but not just any food. We need the right mix of nutrients to stay healthy. Without good nutrition, our bodies get weak, our minds get foggy, and we get sick more easily. Our lives work the same way. Just like a car needs regular oil changes and tune-ups to keep running smoothly, we need regular self-care to keep going. If you skip car maintenance, small problems turn into big, expensive repairs. If you skip self-care, stress builds up until something breaks down.

Finding Your Balance Point

Creating balance means looking at all parts of your life and making sure each gets the attention it needs. When work or school takes all your time and energy, your personal life suffers. When personal problems take over, your responsibilities pile up. True balance means taking care of your mental and emotional needs while managing all areas of your life.

Learning to say "no" is a big part of balance. You need clear boundaries between different parts of your life. Maybe you decide that after 7 PM is family time, or Sunday mornings are just for you. These boundaries protect each part of your life from taking over the others.

Regular breaks and fun activities are like fuel for your mind and spirit. Exercise, hobbies, or just a few minutes of quiet breathing can refill your emotional tank. Without these breaks, you're always running on empty, which leads to burnout.

Remember, balance isn't something you achieve once and forget about. Life keeps changing, and your balance needs change too. Stay flexible and adjust as needed. The goal is to create a life where work and personal time support each other instead of fighting for your attention.

There are signs you can look for to see if you might need more balance in your life. This list doesn't include everything, and you don't need to have all the signs to benefit from adding more balance. Use this list as a guide to help you think about whether you might need to focus more on balance to feel better overall.

Balance is not something
you find, it's
something you create.
Jana Kingsford

Work-Life Balance

Deficiency Level

One sign that something might be off in your life is when one area gets more of your time, energy, and emotions than others. Often, work is the part that takes over, but sometimes, it's your personal life that becomes too demanding. It's important to consider yourself in all of this. Balance means making sure there's time for you, too. Recognizing when you're out of balance is key to knowing when you need to make a change. When things are out of balance, it can affect your relationships with friends and family, make you doubt your abilities, and change how you feel about handling things in your life.

What would this look like for you? :

_____

_____

_____

Consider the reason why this would be a deficiency for you?

_____

_____

_____

What are the supportive reason improve this self care supplement?

_____

_____

_____

Over Commitment

Sometimes, it's easy to ignore a lack of balance because you're focused on being productive and getting things done. But taking on too many tasks, even if it feels productive, can cause you to miss out on important self-care and upset your balance. To check how balanced you are, look at how many tasks you have each day. Are you doing more than you need to, or more than what's necessary to handle your responsibilities?

Think about whether doing so much has just become a habit. Ask yourself: if you did fewer tasks, what would happen? Would it really make a difference? It's important to realize that always doing more isn't always better, and sometimes cutting back can give you more time for yourself. By focusing on what matters and letting go of extra tasks, you can maintain a healthier balance and take better care of yourself.

Deficiency Level

Reflect:

_____

_____

_____

_____

What would this look like for you? :

_____

_____

Consider the reason why this would be a deficiency for you?

_____

_____

What are the supportive reason improve this self care supplement?

_____

_____

Additional Notes:

_____

_____

_____

_____

_____

_____

Time Management Issues

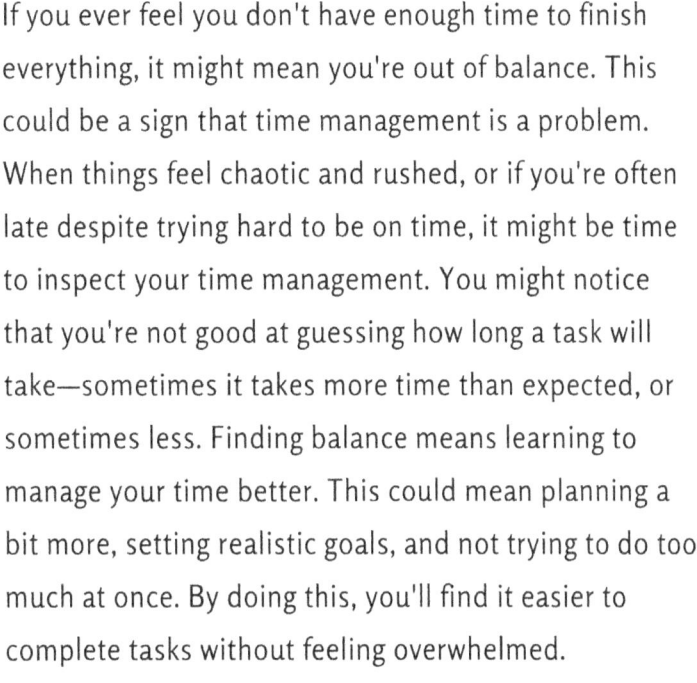

Deficiency Level

If you ever feel you don't have enough time to finish everything, it might mean you're out of balance. This could be a sign that time management is a problem. When things feel chaotic and rushed, or if you're often late despite trying hard to be on time, it might be time to inspect your time management. You might notice that you're not good at guessing how long a task will take—sometimes it takes more time than expected, or sometimes less. Finding balance means learning to manage your time better. This could mean planning a bit more, setting realistic goals, and not trying to do too much at once. By doing this, you'll find it easier to complete tasks without feeling overwhelmed.

Reflect:

_____

_____

_____

_____

_____

What would this look like for you? :

_____

_____

_____

Consider the reason why this would be a deficiency for you?

_____

_____

_____

What are the supportive reason improve this self care supplement?

_____

_____

_____

Additional Notes:

_____

_____

_____

_____

_____

_____

Neglecting Personal Needs

When you're out of balance, you might not have time for your own needs. Taking care of yourself is important and ignoring this can lead to problems. Think about times when you've given up something you wanted to do just to help someone else. How often does this happen to you? If it happens a lot, it could mean you're losing balance in your life. Taking care of your own needs is just as important as helping others.

Deficiency Level

What would this look like for you? :

_____

_____

_____

Consider the reason why this would be a deficiency for you?

_____

_____

_____

What are the supportive reason improve this self care supplement?

_____

_____

_____

Emotional Instability

Deficiency Level

Watch how you react to your emotions. If your life is out of balance, it can affect how you feel emotionally. Everything you do each day affects your emotions. If you give too much emotionally without getting enough back, it can change how you deal with your feelings. You might react differently and wondering why you responded in a certain way when it wasn't necessary. It's important to ensure there's a good balance between giving and receiving emotionally.

What would this look like for you? :

_____

_____

Consider the reason why this would be a deficiency for you?

_____

_____

What are the supportive reason improve this self care supplement?

_____

_____

Diminished Quality of Relationships

Deficiency Level

Changes in our relationships can show we might be missing out on important self-care Vitamin B for balance. Life can pull us in many directions every day. There are always things we need to take care of, but if we're not careful, our relationships can suffer if we don't give them enough attention. Pay attention to how much time you spend with important people in your life. Has the energy or quality of your time together changed? Spending a lot of time with someone doesn't help if the time isn't meaningful. It's about making sure the time you spend together matters.

Reflect:

_____

_____

_____

_____

_____

What would this look like for you? :

_____

_____

Consider the reason why this would be a deficiency for you?

_____

_____

What are the supportive reason improve this self care supplement?

_____

_____

Additional Notes:

_____

_____

_____

_____

_____

_____

Health Neglience

Deficiency Level

When you're very busy, your health might not get the attention it needs. Your sleep might be irregular, leaving you tired. With a hectic schedule, you might not have time for healthy meals. Exercise becomes just the movement you do during the day instead of a planned activity. How your body feels often shows how well you're taking care of yourself. If you're feeling worn out, it might be time to focus more on your health.

What would this look like for you? :

_____

_____

Consider the reason why this would be a deficiency for you?

_____

_____

What are the supportive reason improve this self care supplement?

_____

_____

Vitamin B Supplemental Activities

To help you find activities that keep your Vitamin B for balance strong, think about things that create balance in your life. Make sure you're not spending all your energy on just one part of your life. Choose activities that help you recharge during the day, so you don't feel worn out by the end. These activities also help you notice how your daily tasks might affect your mental health.

Balance is the key to everything. What we do, think, say, eat, feel, they all require awareness and through this awareness we can grow."
Koi Fresco

Time Managment

Think about how you manage your day and activities. We often see time management as just getting tasks done or showing up for appointments on time. But it's also important to think about how these tasks affect you mentally and emotionally. Pay attention to which tasks drain your energy and when they happen during your day. If you have mentally tiring tasks scheduled when you're already feeling low on energy, it might be a good idea to rearrange when you do them. Remember, a task can be mentally draining even if it doesn't take a lot of time. Here are some time management tools that might help you organize your day better.

Reflect:

_____

_____

_____

_____

_____

Frequency you look to participate in this activity:

Daily   ··········   Weekly   ···········   Monthly   ···········   Yearly

Time allotted to spend for this activity:

_____

What what ways will this activity support your mental well-being?

_____

_____

_____

_____

Create a value statement for what you are looking to gain by participating in this activity?

66 ————————————————————————————

_____ 𝅘𝅥𝅮

Additional Notes:

_____

_____

_____

Time Blocking

Try using an hourly calendar to plan out your tasks and how long they might take. Then, use different colors to highlight them based on how you might feel when doing them. You can also use a rating scale to show how mentally tiring each task might be, using a scale from not tiring to very tiring. You don't have to do this every time you make a schedule, but doing it occasionally can help you see how your tasks affect you mentally and emotionally. This way, you can make sure you're balancing your schedule in a way that works better for you.

Reflect:

_____

_____

_____

_____

_____

_____

Frequency you look to participate in this activity:

Daily ·········· Weekly ··········· Monthly ··········· Yearly

Time allotted to spend for this activity:

> [blank box]

What what ways will this activity support your mental well-being?

_____

_____

_____

_____

Create a value statement for what you are looking to gain by participating in this activity?

66 _____

_____ 99

Additional Notes:

_____

_____

_____

To Do List vs.
Calendar Schedule

Keep track of what you want to accomplish each day. Whether you like using a to-do list to check off tasks or marking them on a calendar, make sure it's a useful tool for managing your daily activities. Balance happens when you understand what affects your energy, emotions, and thoughts throughout the day.

Reflect:

_____

_____

_____

_____

_____

_____

_____

_____

Frequency you look to participate in this activity:

Daily   ·········   Weekly   ···········   Monthly   ···········   Yearly

Time allotted to spend for this activity:

```
┌─────────────────────────────────────┐
│                                     │
│                                     │
└─────────────────────────────────────┘
```

What what ways will this activity support your mental well-being?

_____

_____

_____

_____

Create a value statement for what you are looking to gain by participating in this activity?

66 —————————————————————————

ᵒᵒ

Additional Notes:

_____

_____

_____

Set Boundaries

Setting boundaries can help you manage your time and energy better. One way to set boundaries is by deciding what you say "yes" or "no" to. This helps you avoid taking on too many responsibilities. Another way is to pay attention to when and where people or tasks fit into your day. Some people you meet can affect how you feel mentally and emotionally. Noticing this and setting limits on how you interact with them can be helpful.

Reflect:

_____

_____

_____

_____

_____

_____

_____

_____

Frequency you look to participate in this activity:

Daily   ··········   Weekly   ···········   Monthly   ···········   Yearly

Time allotted to spend for this activity:

What what ways will this activity support your mental well-being?

_____

_____

_____

_____

Create a value statement for what you are looking to gain by participating in this activity?

66 ———————————————————————

❞

Additional Notes:

_____

_____

_____

Mindful Breaks

When you have a lot to do, it's easy to forget to take breaks. But breaks are important! Try to schedule brief breaks for yourself on your calendar. You can choose how you want to spend them. Maybe you sit at your desk, take a pause, and enjoy a drink while looking around. Or you could take your time walking to the bathroom and back. If you have more time, you could go for a walk outside, get some fresh air, and check in with your feelings and thoughts. The goal is to have moments in your day where you take a break to balance your mental and emotional energy.

Reflect:

_____

_____

_____

_____

_____

_____

Frequency you look to participate in this activity:

Daily   ··········   Weekly   ···········   Monthly   ···········   Yearly

Time allotted to spend for this activity:

_____

What what ways will this activity support your mental well-being?

_____

_____

_____

_____

Create a value statement for what you are looking to gain by participating in this activity?

66

99

Additional Notes:

_____

_____

_____

S E L F   C A R E   V I T A M I N   B

D e f e c i e n c y   A s s e s s m e n t

Instructions: For each statement, check the number that best describes how often this is true for you.

Rating Scale:

1 = Never/Rarely 2 = Sometimes 3 = Often 4 = Always/Almost Always

---

PART 1: Time Management	1	2	3	4
1. I finish my daily tasks without feeling rushed or overwhelmed.				
2. I accurately estimate how long tasks will take me.				
3. I have enough time for both responsibilities and fun activities.				
4. I arrive on time to appointments and commitments.				
5. I take regular breaks during work or study sessions.				

Part 1   Score: ___/20

PART 2: Energy Distribution	1	2	3	4
6. My energy lasts throughout the day without major crashes.				
7. I have energy left for personal interests after work/school.				
8. I balance high-energy tasks with restful activities.				
9. I know my peak energy times and plan accordingly.				
10. Different areas of my life get appropriate amounts of my energy.				

Part 2   Score: ___/20

PART 3: Boundaries & Commitments	1	2	3	4
11. I comfortably say "no" to requests when I'm already busy.				
12. I avoid overcommitting myself to too many activities.				
13. I protect my personal time from work or school demands.				
14. People respect my boundaries when I set them.				
15. I delegate tasks or ask for help when needed.				

Part 3   Score: ___/20

PART 4: Life Domain Balance	1	2	3	4
16. I spend quality time with family and friends regularly.				
17. I make time for hobbies and activities I enjoy.				
18. My work/school life doesn't overtake my personal life.				
19. I maintain my physical health (sleep, eating, exercise).				
20. I have time for both productivity and relaxation.				

Part 4   Score: ___/20

PART 5: Stress & Emotional Balance	1	2	3	4
21. I manage daily stress without feeling overwhelmed.				
22. My emotions feel stable rather than up and down.				
23. I bounce back quickly from setbacks or bad days.				
24. I have healthy ways to release stress and tension.				
25. I feel in control of my life rather than controlled by it.				

Part 5   Score: ___/20

Calculate Your Total Vitamin B Level:

Add all five part scores: _____/100

Understanding Your Results:

Total Score 80-100: Excellent Balance - Vitamin B Strong!

You've mastered the art of balance! Your life has good rhythm and flow. You manage time well and know your limits. Keep up these great habits and maybe help others find their balance too.

Your focus: Maintain your balance and adapt as life changes.

Total Score 60-79: Good Balance - Vitamin B Adequate

You're doing well with balance but have some wobbly moments. Some areas of life might get too much or too little attention. You're on the right track!

Your focus: Fine-tune problem areas and strengthen your boundaries.

Total Score 40-59: Shaky Balance - Vitamin B Needs Boost

Life often feels like a juggling act where balls keep dropping. You might swing between being too busy and feeling guilty for resting. Time to recalibrate!

Your focus: Start with basic time management and learn to say no.

Total Score Under 40: Poor Balance - Vitamin B Deficiency

You're likely feeling overwhelmed, exhausted, or pulled in too many directions. Life might feel out of control. Don't worry—balance is a skill you can learn!

Your focus: Begin with one small boundary and build from there.

Check Your Warning Signs:

Put a check next to any that apply to you:

☐ I often work/study through lunch or breaks

☐ I can't remember the last time I did something just for fun

☐ I feel guilty when I'm not being productive

☐ My to-do list never seems to get shorter

☐ I'm usually doing several things at once

☐ Weekends feel like catch-up time, not rest time

☐ I rarely have time for exercise or healthy meals

☐ I check work/school messages during personal time

☐ People often comment that I look tired or stressed

☐ I've canceled fun plans because of work/responsibilities

If you checked 5 or more: You definitely need a Vitamin B boost!

Your Lowest Section Score:

Which section scored lowest? Start there:

Lowest: Time Management? → Try: Time blocking, realistic scheduling, buffer time between tasks

Lowest: Energy Distribution? → Try: Energy mapping, matching tasks to energy levels, power naps

Lowest: Boundaries & Commitments? → Try: Practice saying no, communication scripts, commitment inventory

Lowest: Life Domain Balance? → Try: Weekly planning for all life areas, non-negotiable personal time

Lowest: Stress & Emotional Balance? → Try: Daily stress relief, emotion regulation techniques, regular breaks

Your Personal Balance Prescription:

Based on your score, here's your balance-building plan:

Score 80-100: Maintain daily practices + monthly balance check-in

Score 60-79: 15 minutes daily planning + weekly schedule review

Score 40-59: 10 minutes morning planning + 5 minutes evening review + one "no" daily

Score Under 40: Start with 5 minutes daily planning + one boundary this week

Balance Building Activities:

Choose TWO to start this week:

Quick Wins (5 minutes):

☐ Write tomorrow's top 3 priorities tonight

☐ Set a phone alarm for break time

☐ Practice saying "Let me check my schedule"

☐ Do a daily energy check (rate 1-10)

Medium Investment (15 minutes):

☐ Create a weekly schedule including fun time

☐ List all commitments and cut one

☐ Plan tomorrow hour by hour

☐ Take a real lunch break

Bigger Steps (30+ minutes):

☐ Do a complete life audit - what's taking too much/too little time?

☐ Create boundaries for work/personal time

☐ Schedule a weekly "me time" appointment

☐ Design your ideal balanced week

Your Balance Action Plan:

My biggest balance challenge is:

One boundary I will set this week:

Time I will protect for myself:

One commitment I could let go of:

My balance buddy (for accountability):

Weekly Balance Tracker:

Rate each day's balance (1-10): Monday: ___ Tuesday: ___ Wednesday: ___

Thursday: ___ Friday: ___ Weekend: ___

What patterns do you notice?

Remember: Balance doesn't mean equal time for everything. It means the RIGHT amount of time for what matters to you. Some days will tip one way or another—that's normal. The goal is overall balance, not perfect daily balance.

My Vitamin B Goal for This Week:

_____

_____

_____

Date: _____   Initial Score: _____

Emergency Balance Reset:

When you feel off-balance, ask yourself:
1. What's taking more energy than it's giving back?
2. What important thing am I neglecting?
3. What can I say no to right now?
4. What would 10% better balance look like today?

Your balanced life is waiting—start building it one boundary at a time!

Connection
is why we're here

Build meaningful relationships
that nourish your soul.

4 Self-Care Vitamin C - Connection

Think about the last time you spent time with someone and walked away feeling truly happy and understood. That warm, fulfilled feeling is what Vitamin C for Connection is all about. We interact with people all day long—buying coffee, chatting with classmates or coworkers, talking to family about our day. But not all interactions create real connections. Sometimes we're so busy that we rush through these moments without really being present.

What Makes a Connection Meaningful?

When most people think about meaningful connections, family comes to mind first. Family gives us that ongoing sense of support and belonging. Knowing you have people who are always part of your life feels good. But here's the challenge: we need to move beyond just being around family to actually connecting with them.

Look at your typical family interactions. Often, we're focused on tasks —running errands, doing chores, discussing schedules. While these things need to happen, they can become chances for deeper connection. That trip to the grocery store with your spouse? It could be quality time to talk and laugh together. Helping your child with homework? It's a chance to show you care. The key is seeing these everyday moments as opportunities, not just chores.

When we miss the connection opportunity in daily tasks, everything feels like work. We get annoyed and uninterested. But when we recognize that these activities can strengthen our relationships, even boring errands become more enjoyable. It's all about changing how we see things.

Signs You Need More Vitamin C

We are hardwired to connect with others, it's what gives purpose and meaning to our lives.
Brené Brown

Social Isolation

Deficiency Level

If you're spending a lot less time with others than usual, it might be a sign something is off. This isn't about whether you're an extrovert or introvert. People often think being introverted means not liking social interaction, but that's not true. Introverts enjoy connecting; they just prefer smaller, more meaningful interactions instead of big groups. To see if you're missing out on social connections, think about what your usual level of social activity is and check if you're doing less than what feels normal for you.

What would this look like for you? :

_____

_____

_____

Consider the reason why this would be a deficiency for you?

_____

_____

_____

What are the supportive reason improve this self care supplement?

_____

_____

Loneliness

Deficiency Level

Loneliness is interesting because you can feel it even when people are around. It's about whether your interactions make you feel connected. The important thing is to think about not just if you've spent time with friends or family, but if you felt heard, understood, and valued during those times. Those are the feelings that help us feel really connected.

What would this look like for you? :

_____

_____

_____

Consider the reason why this would be a deficiency for you?

_____

_____

_____

What are the supportive reason improve this self care supplement?

_____

_____

_____

Communication Challenges

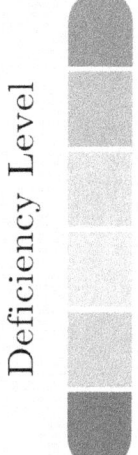

Deficiency Level

If you're finding it hard to share your thoughts and feelings, it might mean you're not feeling connected enough. Communicating is a skill that gets better with practice. When you spend less time with people who make you feel connected, you have fewer chances to use that skill. If you can't explain what's happening in your life easily, it might be a sign that you need some self-care to help you feel more connected to others.

What would this look like for you? :

_____

_____

Consider the reason why this would be a deficiency for you?

_____

_____

What are the supportive reason improve this self care supplement?

_____

_____

Weak Support Systems

Deficiency Level

Sometimes, we think about who our support people are. This might happen if we feel like we don't have enough people to turn to, or if it's been a long time since we've needed their help, and we're unsure if they're still there for us. Recognizing this lack of connection is important because having a support system is a big part of feeling connected. It's helpful to know who the key people are that you can rely on and what types of things they can help with.

What would this look like for you? :

_____

_____

_____

Consider the reason why this would be a deficiency for you?

_____

_____

_____

What are the supportive reason improve this self care supplement?

_____

_____

_____

Emotionally Unavailable

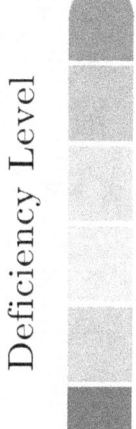

Deficiency Level

If you notice changes in how you express your feelings in relationships, it might mean you're lacking connection and need to spend more time with others. Maybe you're not sharing your emotions openly, or you act differently from how you truly feel. It could also be hard for you to connect with others' experiences. These changes in emotions with people around you can show that you're not feeling as connected as you could be.

What would this look like for you? :

_____

_____

Consider the reason why this would be a deficiency for you?

_____

_____

What are the supportive reason improve this self care supplement?

_____

_____

Vitamin C Supplemental Activities

When thinking about activities for Vitamin C for Connection, remember they should support making and keeping relationships that help you feel good. Life can be busy, and even if you're around people a lot, it doesn't always mean you're really connecting with them. Look for activities where you not only spend time with others but also feel heard, understood, and appreciated. This makes connections meaningful.

Being deeply loved by someone gives you strength, while loving someone deeply gives you courage.
Lao Tzu

Quality Time with Key People

It's important to know which people are worth connecting with and how both of you benefit from spending time together. Start by figuring out who these key people are and think about how you feel after being with them. Once you know this, you can plan when, where, and how often to connect with them. Consider which part of your life needs more connection. If you feel disconnected from family, focus on those relationships. If it's more about individual friendships, then spend time with friends who make you feel connected. Sometimes, it's about work connections too, so think about who and why you need to connect in your professional life.

Reflect:

_____

_____

_____

_____

Frequency you look to participate in this activity:

Daily ········· Weekly ·········· Monthly ·········· Yearly

Time allotted to spend for this activity:

What what ways will this activity support your mental well-being?

_____

_____

_____

_____

Create a value statement for what you are looking to gain by participating in this activity?

❝

❞

Additional Notes:

_____

_____

_____

Practice Being Presentr

Being present in the moment is all about focusing on what's happening now. To really enjoy your time connecting with someone, try to stay focused on them. It might feel like just when you're connecting, something distracts you. To make your time together special, think about how to block out these distractions. Pay attention to the conversation or activity you're doing with them. Also, remember to show each other that you value the time you are spending together and appreciate each other's company.

Reflect:

_____

_____

_____

_____

_____

Frequency you look to participate in this activity:

Daily ·········· Weekly ··········· Monthly ··········· Yearly

Time allotted to spend for this activity:

_____

What what ways will this activity support your mental well-being?

_____

_____

_____

_____

Create a value statement for what you are looking to gain by participating in this activity?

❝ _____

_____ ❞

Additional Notes:

_____

_____

_____

Join a Club or Group

Sometimes, you may want to meet new people, either socially or for work. Consider joining a group or club that matches your interests, like a book club or hiking club. This way, you can connect with others who enjoy the same things. Sometimes, you might like activities that your current friends or family aren't into, which can feel lonely. But by joining a group, you can find people who understand and share your interests. Plus, being part of a group can help you grow personally or professionally. Things like masterminds or networking groups are great for making new connections and learning new things.

Reflect:

_____

_____

_____

_____

_____

Frequency you look to participate in this activity:

Daily ·········· Weekly ··········· Monthly ··········· Yearly

Time allotted to spend for this activity:

What what ways will this activity support your mental well-being?

_____

_____

_____

_____

Create a value statement for what you are looking to gain by participating in this activity?

❝

❞

Additional Notes:

_____

_____

_____

Start small. Pick one connection goal for this week. Maybe it's putting your phone away during dinner or asking a friend how they're really doing (and listening to the answer). Small steps lead to big changes.
Track your progress. Notice how different interactions make you feel. Energy boost? That's a good connection. Exhausted afterward? Maybe that relationship needs boundaries.

Be patient. Building real connections takes time. Some conversations will be awkward. Some attempts won't work out. That's normal and okay. Keep trying.

The Connection Ripple Effect

When you strengthen your connections, amazing things happen. You feel less stressed because you have support. Your confidence grows because people value you. You laugh more, worry less, and feel like you belong.

Plus, your positive connections inspire others. When you're fully present with someone, they often respond by being more present too. When you share genuinely, others feel safe to do the same. You create a ripple effect of real connection.

Remember: humans are wired for connection. It's not a luxury or something only extroverts need. It's as essential as food and sleep. By taking care of your Vitamin C needs, you're not just improving your own life

—you're making the world a little less lonely, one genuine interaction at a time.

Your connections don't need to be perfect. They just need to be real. So put down this book, look around, and ask someone how they're doing. Then really listen to the answer. That's where connection begins.

The greatest gift you can
give someone is your time,
your attention,
your love, your concern.
Joel Osteen

SELF CARE VITAMIN C

Defeciency Assessment

Instructions: For each statement, check the number that best describes how often this is true for you.

Rating Scale:

1 = Never/Rarely 2 = Sometimes 3 = Often 4 = Always/Almost Always

PART 1: Quality of Connections	1	2	3	4
1. I have people in my life who truly understand me.				
2. After spending time with others, I feel energized and happy.				
3. I feel comfortable being my authentic self around others.				
4. My relationships involve equal give and take.				
5. I have deep, meaningful conversations beyond surface topics.				

Part 1   Score: ___/20

PART 2: Communication & Expression	1	2	3	4
6. I share my true feelings with people I trust.				
7. I'm comfortable asking for help when I need it.				
8. I express appreciation and gratitude to others.				
9. I can talk about problems without attacking or withdrawing.				
10. People tell me I'm a good listener.				

Part 2   Score: ___/20

PART 3: Social Engagement	1	2	3	4
11. I regularly spend quality time with friends or family.				
12. I make an effort to stay in touch with people I care about.				
13. I participate in group activities or shared interests.				
14. I'm open to meeting new people and making friends.				
15. I balance alone time with social time effectively.				

Part 3   Score: ___/20

PART 4: Support System	1	2	3	4
16. I have people I can count on in tough times.				
17. I know who to call when I need different types of support.				
18. I offer support to others when they need it.				
19. I feel like I belong somewhere (family, friends, community).				
20. People check in on me, and I check in on them.				

Part 4   Score: ___/20

PART 5: Emotional Connection	1	2	3	4
21. I feel genuinely cared about by others.				
22. Physical affection (hugs, high-fives) is part of my life.				
23. I celebrate successes and joys with others.				
24. I can be vulnerable without fear of judgment.				
25. My relationships help me grow as a person.				

Part 5   Score: ___/20

Calculate Your Total Vitamin C Level:

Add all five part scores: _____/100

Understanding Your Results:

Total Score 80-100: Rich Connections - Vitamin C Strong!

You have fulfilling, supportive relationships! You've built meaningful connections and know how to maintain them. Your social life energizes you. Keep nurturing these bonds!

Your focus: Maintain current relationships and model healthy connection for others.

Total Score 60-79: Good Connections - Vitamin C Adequate

You have solid relationships with room to deepen. Some connections are strong while others might be surface-level. You're on a good path!

Your focus: Deepen existing relationships and strengthen communication skills.

Total Score 40-59: Limited Connections - Vitamin C Needs Boost

You might feel lonely even with people around. Connections often stay surface-level or feel draining. Time to invest in relationship building!

Your focus: Start with one or two relationships to strengthen and practice vulnerability.

Total Score Under 40: Isolation Risk - Vitamin C Deficiency

You're likely feeling disconnected and unsupported. Building connections might feel scary or impossible. Remember—everyone needs connection, including you!

Your focus: Begin with small steps like texting one person or joining one activity.

Connection Red Flags (Check any that apply):

☐ I often feel lonely even in a crowd

☐ Most conversations stay on surface topics (weather, work, etc.)

☐ I pretend everything's fine when it's not

☐ I haven't had a real hug in weeks

☐ No one really knows what's going on in my life

☐ I give much more than I receive in relationships

☐ I avoid social situations because they drain me

☐ I can't remember the last time I laughed with someone

☐ I have hundreds of online "friends" but no one to call

☐ I feel like no one would notice if I disappeared

If you checked 4 or more: Your Vitamin C needs immediate attention!

Your Lowest Section Score:

Target your lowest scoring area first:

Lowest: Quality of Connections? → Try: One-on-one time, deeper conversations, authenticity practice

Lowest: Communication & Expression? → Try: Feeling check-ins, active listening, "I feel" statements

Lowest: Social Engagement? → Try: Regular friend dates, joining groups, reaching out more

Lowest: Support System? → Try: Identifying support needs, building reciprocal help habits

Lowest: Emotional Connection? →

Your Connection Prescription:

Based on your score, follow this connection-building plan:

Score 80-100: Maintain weekly meaningful connections + mentor others

Score 60-79: 2-3 quality interactions weekly + deepen one relationship

Score 40-59: Daily connection practice + weekly meaningful conversation

Score Under 40: One small daily connection + professional support consideration

Connection Building Activities:

Choose your starting point based on comfort level:

Baby Steps (for shy or anxious):

☐ Text one person "thinking of you"

☐ Smile and say hi to three people today

☐ Comment genuinely on someone's social media

☐ Ask one person "How are you really?"

Small Steps (building confidence):

☐ Have a 10-minute phone call with someone

☐ Invite someone for coffee or a walk

☐ Share one real feeling with a trusted person

☐ Join an online group about your interests

Bigger Steps (ready to connect):

☐ Plan a regular meetup with friends

☐ Join an in-person club or class

☐ Host a small gathering at your home

☐ Have a heart-to-heart conversation

Brave Steps (deepening connection):

☐ Share a fear or struggle with someone

☐ Ask for help with something specific

☐ Tell someone how much they mean to you

☐ Repair a relationship that needs attention

Your Connection Types Inventory

Rate the quality of your connections (0 = none, 5 = excellent):

Family: ___ Close Friends: ___ Casual Friends: ___ Work/School

Relationships: ___ Community/Neighbors: ___ Online Connections: ___

Mentor/Mentee: ___ Romantic (if applicable): ___

Where do you need more connection?

Weekly Connection Planner:

Plan one meaningful connection for each day:

Monday:

Tuesday:

Wednesday:

Thursday:

Friday:

Saturday:

Sunday:

Conversation Starters for Deeper Connection:

When surface talk gets old, try:

- "What's really going on with you lately?"
- "What's been the highlight of your week?"
- "What's something you're struggling with?"
- "What are you excited about right now?"
- "How can I support you better?"
- "What's something you've been thinking about lately?"

Your Support Network Map:

Write names of people you can turn to for:

Emotional Support (crying, venting):

Practical Help (rides, moving, tasks):

Fun and Laughter:

Advice and Wisdom:

Celebrating Success:

Gaps to fill:

Connection Maintenance Checklist:

For important relationships, regularly:

☐ Check in beyond "How are you?"

☐ Remember important dates/events

☐ Share your own struggles (appropriately)

☐ Do activities together

☐ Express gratitude and appreciation

☐ Make time when they need you

☐ Celebrate their wins

☐ Accept help when offered

My Connection Commitment:

One relationship I want to strengthen:

How I'll invest in it this week:

One new connection I'd like to make:

My biggest connection fear to overcome:

Someone who might need my connection:

Remember: Connection isn't about having tons of friends—it's about having real relationships that feed your soul. Even one genuine connection can transform your life. Start where you are, and build slowly.

My Vitamin C Goal for This Week:

Date: Initial Score:

Emergency Connection Boost:

When feeling disconnected, try:

1. Reach out to one person right now
2. Give someone a genuine compliment
3. Ask for a hug (or give one)
4. Share one honest feeling
5. Remember: everyone feels lonely sometimes—you're not broken

You deserve meaningful connections. Start building them one conversation at a time!

*Let go of what
no longer serves you.*

RELEASE NEGATIVITY AND
CREATE MENTAL CLARITY

5 Self-Care Vitamin D - Detox

Just like your body needs to get rid of waste and toxins, your mind and emotions need detoxing too. Vitamin D for Detox is about clearing out the negative stuff that weighs you down—bad thoughts, stressful situations, toxic relationships, and emotional baggage. Think of it as spring cleaning for your mental health.

Understanding Mental and Emotional Detox

When we talk about detoxing, most people think about physical health. But mental detox is just as important. Every day, we absorb negativity from various sources:

- Stressful news and social media
- Difficult conversations
- Disappointing experiences
- Hurtful comments
- Our own negative thoughts

Without regular mental detox, this negativity builds up like garbage in a house. Eventually, there's no room for positive thoughts and feelings. You feel overwhelmed, exhausted, and stuck.

How Your Body's Natural Detox System Works

Your body has an amazing natural cleaning system. The liver acts like a filter, breaking down harmful substances. The kidneys flush out waste through urine. Your skin releases toxins through sweat. Your lungs exhale waste gases. Your digestive system eliminates what you don't need.

All these parts work together like a team. When one isn't working well, your whole body suffers. The same is true for mental health—you need multiple strategies working together to stay emotionally healthy.

Signs You Need More Vitamin C

A friend is someone who knows all about you and still loves you.
Elbert Hubbard

Emotional Baggage

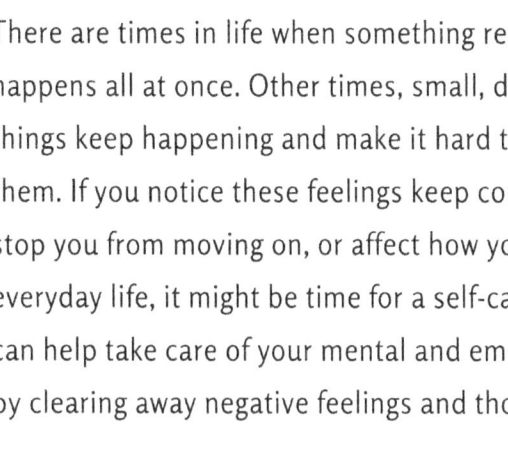

There are times in life when something really hurtful happens all at once. Other times, small, disappointing things keep happening and make it hard to deal with them. If you notice these feelings keep coming back, stop you from moving on, or affect how you handle everyday life, it might be time for a self-care detox. This can help take care of your mental and emotional needs by clearing away negative feelings and thoughts.

What would this look like for you? :

_____

_____

_____

Consider the reason why this would be a deficiency for you?

_____

_____

_____

What are the supportive reason improve this self care supplement?

_____

_____

_____

Chronic Stress or Anxiety

Deficiency Level

You might need a self-care detox activity when you're feeling stressed and overwhelmed because problems are not being dealt with. It could be hard for you to relax and focus on what's happening right now. If stress or anxiety is ignored, it can make it difficult for you to concentrate on the important things.

What would this look like for you? :

_____

_____

_____

Consider the reason why this would be a deficiency for you?

_____

_____

_____

What are the supportive reason improve this self care supplement?

_____

_____

_____

Negative Self-Talk

Deficiency Level

Thinking about ways to improve is one thing, but it's different if all you can see are the things going wrong and not the good stuff. When it's easier to focus on the negative than the positive, it's a sign that you need some self-care. This build-up of negativity shows its time to let go of the bad so you can enjoy the good things.

What would this look like for you? :

_____

_____

_____

Consider the reason why this would be a deficiency for you?

_____

_____

_____

What are the supportive reason improve this self care supplement?

_____

_____

_____

Unhealthy Relationships

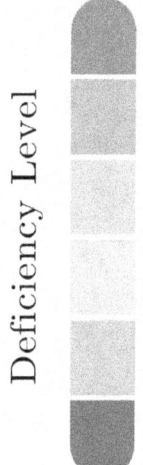

Deficiency Level

It's important to look occasionally at the relationships in your life. It's tough to see when change is needed in long-term relationships, and even harder to decide if you need to limit how much access certain people have to you. If a relationship feels toxic, draining, or one-sided, it might be time for a change. Setting boundaries in these situations can be difficult, but sometimes it's necessary for your well-being.

What would this look like for you? :

_____

_____

_____

Consider the reason why this would be a deficiency for you?

_____

_____

_____

What are the supportive reason improve this self care supplement?

_____

_____

_____

Persistent Emotional Fatigue

Deficiency Level

Your emotions can get tired, just like your body. Sometimes, you might face one stressful thing after another without getting a break to recover emotionally. If you don't have time to rest from these emotional demands, you can end up feeling exhausted. Emotional fatigue might make you feel unmotivated or unable to enjoy things you usually like.

What would this look like for you? :

_____

_____

_____

Consider the reason why this would be a deficiency for you?

_____

_____

_____

What are the supportive reason improve this self care supplement?

_____

_____

_____

Vitamin D Supplemental Activities

To really enjoy healthy activities, you sometimes need to clear away the negative stuff first. Detoxing with self-care activities means getting rid of things that affect you in a bad way. This could mean focusing on getting rid of negative thoughts and feelings. Other times, it might mean staying away from negative situations, people, or past events. Sometimes you might need to remove these things completely, and other times you just need to limit how often they happen. The big idea is that being around unhealthy influences can make it hard to enjoy and experience the good things in life.

Clutter is not just physical
stuff. It's old ideas,
toxic relationships,
and bad habits.
Eleanor Brown

Two Step Detox Process

Step 1: Stop Taking in Toxins

First, reduce what negativity you absorb:

Digital Boundaries:

- Limit social media time
- Unfollow accounts that make you feel bad
- Take regular phone breaks
- Avoid negative news before bed

People Boundaries:

- Spend less time with draining people
- Say no to conversations that always turn negative
- Avoid gossip and complaint sessions
- Choose supportive friends

Mental Boundaries:

- Challenge negative thoughts when they appear
- Refuse to dwell on what you can't control
- Focus on present moments, not past regrets
- Limit comparing yourself to others

Two Step Detox Process

Step 2: Remove What's Already Built Up

Next, clear out existing negativity:

Brain Dump Journaling: This isn't pretty writing or keeping memories. It's mental trash removal:

1. Get paper you can throw away
2. Write down everything bothering you
3. Don't worry about grammar or making sense
4. Focus on release, not complaining
5. When done, rip it up or delete it

Physical Release:

- Exercise to sweat out stress
- Cry when you need to—tears release stress hormones
- Scream into a pillow
- Take walks in nature

Creative Expression:

- Draw or paint your feelings
- Write songs or poetry
- Build or create something

Frequency you look to participate in this activity:

Daily ·········· Weekly ·········· Monthly ·········· Yearly

Time allotted to spend for this activity:

What what ways will this activity support your mental well-being?

_____

_____

_____

_____

Create a value statement for what you are looking to gain by participating in this activity?

66 _____

_____ 66

Additional Notes:

_____

_____

_____

Brain Dump Journal

A helpful way to journal is through a brain dump approach. This type of journaling is a bit different because it focuses on detoxing your mind. Instead of keeping what you write to look back on later, the goal here is to get rid of those thoughts. It's best to write on something you can delete or throw away. Also, focus on letting go of thoughts rather than just complaining. Your writing should reflect the idea of releasing what's on your mind. This process is about clearing your mind, so it's important to remember that your goal is to detox.

Reflect:

_____

_____

_____

_____

_____

Frequency you look to participate in this activity:

Daily .... Weekly .... Monthly .... Yearly

Time allotted to spend for this activity:

```
┌─────────────────────────────────────┐
│                                     │
│                                     │
└─────────────────────────────────────┘
```

What what ways will this activity support your mental well-being?

_____

_____

_____

_____

Create a value statement for what you are looking to gain by participating in this activity?

66 ——

_____ 🎵🎵

Additional Notes:

_____

_____

_____

Professional Supports

Sometimes, emotional toxins are too deep or complex to handle alone. Consider professional help if:

- Negative feelings last for weeks without improvement
- Past trauma keeps affecting your daily life
- You can't stop certain thought patterns
- Anxiety or sadness interferes with school, work, or relationships
- You've tried self-help but still feel stuck

Therapists, counselors, and coaches are like professional detox specialists for your mind. They have tools and techniques you can't access on your own.

Reflect:

_____

_____

_____

_____

_____

Frequency you look to participate in this activity:

Daily ·········· Weekly ··········· Monthly ··········· Yearly

Time allotted to spend for this activity:

```
┌────────────────────────────────────┐
│                                    │
│                                    │
└────────────────────────────────────┘
```

What what ways will this activity support your mental well-being?

_____

_____

_____

_____

Create a value statement for what you are looking to gain by participating in this activity?

66 ————————————————————————————————

                                                                      99

Additional Notes:

_____

_____

_____

S E L F   C A R E   V I T A M I N   D

D e f e c i e n c y   A s s e s s m e n t

Instructions: For each statement, check the number that best describes how often this is true for you.

Rating Scale:

1 = Never/Rarely 2 = Sometimes 3 = Often 4 = Always/Almost Always

PART 1:Digital & Environmental Detox	1	2	3	4
1. I take regular breaks from screens and devices.				
2. My living/work space is organized and calming.				
3. I limit exposure to negative news and social media.				
4. I can disconnect from technology without feeling anxious.				
5. My environment supports peace rather than stress.				

Part 1   Score: ___/20

PART 2: Mental & Emotional Clarity	1	2	3	4
6. I let go of negative thoughts rather than dwelling on them.				
7. I can identify thoughts that aren't helpful or true.				
8. My mind feels clear and focused, not cluttered.				
9. I release worry about things I cannot control.				
10. I practice forgiveness (of myself and others).				

Part 2   Score: ___/20

PART 3: Toxic Relationship Management	1	2	3	4
11. I limit time with people who drain my energy.				
12. I've set boundaries with negative or toxic people.				
13. I can walk away from harmful conversations or situations.				
14. I protect myself from others' negativity and drama.				
15. I surround myself with positive, supportive people.				

Part 3   Score: ___/20

PART 4: Processing Past Experiences	1	2	3	4
16. I've dealt with past hurts rather than carrying them.				
17. Old memories don't control my current emotions.				
18. I can think about the past without getting stuck there.				
19. I've released grudges and resentments.				
20. I learn from the past without living in it.				

Part 4   Score: ___/20

PART 5: Stress & Negative Energy Release	1	2	3	4
21. I have healthy ways to release stress and tension.				
22. I regularly clear out emotional buildup.				
23. I can calm myself when overwhelmed.				
24. I avoid carrying others' stress as my own.				
25. I end each day feeling mentally refreshed, not drained.				

Part 5   Score: ___/20

Calculate Your Total Vitamin D Level:

Add all five part scores: _____/100

Understanding Your Results:

Total Score 80-100: Clear & Clean - Vitamin D Strong!

Your mental space is well-maintained! You know how to protect yourself from negativity and clear out what doesn't serve you. Keep up these excellent habits!

Your focus: Maintain current practices and help others learn to detox.

Total Score 60-79: Mostly Clear - Vitamin D Good

You're doing well but have some clutter. You can usually manage negativity but sometimes get overwhelmed. You know what to do but don't always do it.

Your focus: Be more consistent with detox practices and strengthen boundaries.

Total Score 40-59: Cluttered Space - Vitamin D Needs Boost

Your mental space feels crowded and heavy. Negativity tends to stick around longer than it should. Time for a good mental cleaning!

Your focus: Start with one area to declutter and build regular detox habits.

Total Score Under 40: Toxic Overload - Vitamin D Deficiency

You're carrying too much mental and emotional weight. Life feels overwhelming and negative. This is affecting your well-being significantly.

Your focus: Begin with small daily releases and consider professional support.

Toxicity Check (Mark all that apply):

☐ I replay negative conversations in my head repeatedly

☐ I can't stop scrolling even when it makes me feel bad

☐ Drama seems to follow me everywhere

☐ I feel responsible for everyone else's problems

☐ My space is so cluttered it stresses me out

☐ I hold onto items connected to painful memories

☐ Certain people always leave me feeling drained

☐ I compare myself to others on social media constantly

☐ Past mistakes haunt my daily thoughts

☐ I absorb news/world events like a sponge

If you checked 5 or more: You urgently need a mental detox!

Your Lowest Section Score:

Focus on your weakest area first:

Lowest: Digital & Environmental? → Try: Screen time limits, decluttering, nature time, clean spaces

Lowest: Mental & Emotional Clarity? → Try: Thought stopping, meditation, positive affirmations, journaling

Lowest: Toxic Relationship Management? → Try: Boundary setting, limited contact, energy vampire identification

Lowest: Processing Past Experiences? → Try: Forgiveness work, therapy, closure rituals, memory reframing

Lowest: Stress & Negative Energy Release? → Try: Physical release, creative expression, breathing exercises

Your Detox Prescription:

Based on your score, here's your cleansing plan:

Score 80-100: Weekly mini-detox + monthly deep cleanse

Score 60-79: Daily 10-minute detox + weekly digital break

Score 40-59: Daily 15-minute release + weekend detox activities

Score Under 40: 2-3 daily detox practices + professional support

Detox Activities Menu:

Choose based on what you need to release:

Quick Daily Detox (5-10 minutes):

☐ Brain dump in a journal (then tear it up) ☐ 5-minute social media timer

☐ Delete 10 items (emails, photos, texts) ☐ Step outside for fresh air

☐ Dance to release energy

Medium Detox (15-30 minutes):

☐ Clean one small space thoroughly

☐ Unfollow negative social media accounts

☐ Write and burn a letter you'll never send

☐ Take a technology-free walk

☐ Practice saying no to one request

Deep Detox (30+ minutes):

☐ Major declutter of living space ☐ Digital detox for full day

☐ End or limit a toxic relationship ☐ Forgiveness meditation

☐ Professional therapy session

Emergency Detox (when overwhelmed):

☐ Leave the situation immediately ☐ Call supportive friend

☐ Intense physical exercise ☐ Scream into pillow

☐ Cold shower reset

Your Balance Action Plan:

My biggest source of mental toxins:

One thing I'll stop taking in:

One thing I need to release:

My daily detox activity will be:

My weekly deep clean will include:

Digital Detox Tracker:

Track your screen time and mood:

Daily Screen Time: Monday: ___ hrs | Mood: ___ Tuesday: ___ hrs | Mood: ___ Wednesday: ___ hrs | Mood: ___ Thursday: ___ hrs | Mood: ___ Friday: ___ hrs | Mood: ___ Weekend: ___ hrs | Mood: ___

Pattern Noticed:

Boundary Setting Scripts:

Practice these phrases:

- "That doesn't work for me"
- "I need to step away from this conversation"
- "I'm taking a break from my phone"
- "I can't take on that problem right now"
- "Let's talk about something positive"
- "I need some space to process"

Mental Space Cleaning Checklist:

Weekly maintenance:

☐ Clear phone photos/apps

☐ Declutter one space

☐ Unsubscribe from negative inputs

☐ Release one worry you can't control

☐ Say no to one draining activity

☐ Brain dump journal session

☐ Do one thing that brings joy

☐ Practice gratitude to shift focus

Energy Vampire Identifier:

My biggest balance challenge is:

Energy Givers (keep more):

Neutral (maintain as is):

My Detox Commitment:

Physical space I'll declutter:

Digital habit I'll change:

Negative thought pattern to release:

Toxic relationship to address:

Daily release ritual I'll practice:

Remember: Detoxing isn't about perfection—it's about regularly clearing what weighs you down. Like taking out the trash, it needs to happen regularly or things get smelly! Start small, be consistent, and notice how much lighter you feel.

My Vitamin D Goal for This Week:

Date: Initial Score:

Quick Detox When Triggered:

1. STOP - Don't react immediately
2. BREATHE - Three deep breaths
3. RELEASE - Shake it out physically
4. REDIRECT - Focus on something positive
5. PROTECT - Reinforce your boundaries

You deserve a clear, peaceful mind. Start creating it one release at a time!

Movement is medicine
for the body and mind.

DISCOVER THE JOY OF MOVEMENT

6 Self-Care Vitamin E - Exercise

Think of exercise as a powerful vitamin for your mind and body. Just like taking daily vitamins keeps you healthy, regular exercise gives your brain and emotions the boost they need. It's not just about getting fit—it's about feeling happier, thinking clearer, and handling life better.

The Magic of Movement

When you exercise, amazing things happen inside your body and brain. Your body releases special chemicals called endorphins—nature's happy pills. These "feel-good" chemicals chase away stress and worry while making you feel joy and calm. It's like your body has its own pharmacy, and exercise is the prescription.

Moving your body also pumps more blood to your brain. This extra blood brings oxygen and nutrients that help you think clearly and focus better. Ever notice how a walk can help you solve a problem? That's your brain getting the fuel it needs to work its best.

Building Confidence Through Movement

Every time you exercise, you prove something to yourself: you're capable. Maybe today you walked a little further than yesterday. Maybe you finally nailed that basketball shot. These small victories build real confidence that spreads to everything else in your life. When you feel strong physically, you feel strong mentally too.

Exercise isn't just a solo activity—it connects you with others. Whether you're on a team, in a class, or just walking with a friend, moving together creates bonds. These connections give you support when times get tough and people to celebrate with when things go well.

Signs You Need More Vitamin E

Movement is a medicine for creating change in a person's physical, emotional, and mental states.
Carol Welch

Physical Fatigue

Deficiency Level

Noticing when you're physically tired can help you know when it's time for self-care. If you still feel tired and slow even after getting enough sleep, or if your energy is always low, it might be a sign you need something more than just rest. While it's easy to think more sleep will fix tiredness, sometimes getting active can actually boost your energy and help your body handle what you need to do. So, a little exercise might be just what you need to feel better and more energetic.

What would this look like for you? :

_____

_____

_____

Consider the reason why this would be a deficiency for you?

_____

_____

_____

What are the supportive reason improve this self care supplement?

_____

_____

_____

Stiffness and Poor Mobility

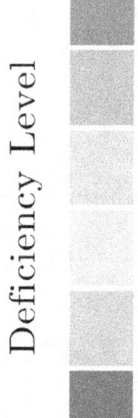

Deficiency Level

If you're feeling stiff or having trouble moving, it might be a sign that you need more exercise. Stiffness, aches, or pains can often happen because you're not moving enough. When life gets busy, exercise is usually one of the first things we skip. But without it, stiffness and discomfort can build up in our bodies. Our daily activities affect how we feel, and without supporting our body's need for flexibility and strength, these issues can show up in unhealthy ways. Exercise helps keep everything moving smoothly and feeling good.

What would this look like for you? :

_____

_____

_____

Consider the reason why this would be a deficiency for you?

_____

_____

_____

What are the supportive reason improve this self care supplement?

_____

_____

_____

Weight Management Issues

Deficiency Level

When we talk about managing weight, we often think about healthy eating and exercise. But weight management is also important for mental and emotional health, not just for boosting self-esteem. Changes in weight can be a sign of depression and anxiety. Noticing these changes helps you understand other factors affecting how your body handles food. Exercising regularly supports your body's natural systems, helping them work well and keeping you healthy.

What would this look like for you? :

_____

_____

_____

Consider the reason why this would be a deficiency for you?

_____

_____

_____

What are the supportive reason improve this self care supplement?

_____

_____

_____

Sleep Problems

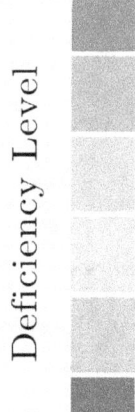

Deficiency Level

Sleep is really important for mental health, and not getting enough can affect how you handle life and relationships. It can be hard to fall asleep, stay asleep, or feel rested because of dreams or overthinking that stops you from getting deep REM sleep. Sometimes, getting more exercise can help you sleep better. Knowing what self-care activities to include can improve how you take care of your mental and emotional health.

What would this look like for you? :

_____

_____

_____

Consider the reason why this would be a deficiency for you?

_____

_____

_____

What are the supportive reason improve this self care supplement?

_____

_____

_____

Cognitive Fog

Deficiency Level

Having trouble thinking clearly can be a sign that your mental and emotional health needs attention. If you're finding it harder to concentrate, solve problems, or you feel slow and tired, it might be time to think about self-care. Exercise can be a great way to help your brain stay strong and meet your mental and emotional needs. It supports your mind and can help you handle life's challenges better.

What would this look like for you? :

_____

_____

_____

Consider the reason why this would be a deficiency for you?

_____

_____

_____

What are the supportive reason improve this self care supplement?

_____

_____

_____

Decreased Strength and Endurance

Deficiency Level

Sometimes, it's tough to get through the physical demands of your day, even if the tasks aren't very hard. What you do every day can affect how your body feels and performs. If you notice it's getting harder to keep up, it might be because your body isn't as strong or prepared for what you need to do, like sitting through long meetings, traveling between places, or standing for a long time. When your body struggles, negative thoughts about your abilities can come up, too. Getting stronger and being able to handle these tasks better might come from adding some exercise to your routine to build physical strength and endurance.

Reflect:

_____

_____

_____

_____

What would this look like for you? :

_____

_____

_____

Consider the reason why this would be a deficiency for you?

_____

_____

_____

What are the supportive reason improve this self care supplement?

_____

_____

_____

Additional Notes:

_____

_____

_____

_____

_____

_____

Vitamin E Supplemental Activities

Now that you understand why your body and mind need Vitamin E, it's time to explore the many ways you can get moving. The beauty of exercise is that there's no one-size-fits-all approach—what works for your best friend might not work for you, and that's perfectly okay. Think of this section as your personal menu of movement options. Some days you might crave the energy of a group activity, other days you'll want the peace of a solo walk. Some people love competition, others prefer calm stretching. The key is finding activities that you actually enjoy, because the best exercise is the one you'll actually do. Let's explore different ways to add movement to your life, so you can discover what makes your body and mind feel their best.

The body benefits from movement, and the mind benefits from stillness.
Sakyong Mipham

Join a Fitness Class or Team Sport

Joining a fitness class or team sport can help you get healthier and make new friends. It's a fun way to stay active while building friendships and emotional support through shared activities. Exercise can also strengthen your body and help it handle stress or emotions better. During a workout, you have a chance to let go of stress and anxiety, which helps you feel better overall.

Frequency you look to participate in this activity:

Daily ·········· Weekly ··········· Monthly ··········· Yearly

Time allotted to spend for this activity:

What what ways will this activity support your mental well-being?

_____

_____

Create a value statement for what you are looking to gain by participating in this activity?

66 _____

_____ 99

Regular Walks or Hiking

Taking regular walks, whether in a park or around your neighborhood, can make you more flexible and strong. This simple activity can give you more energy, clear your mind, and help you manage your weight, making everyday tasks easier. Being outside is also great for your health. If you can, try going on a nature hike, which can make your exercise routine even better.

Frequency you look to participate in this activity:

Daily ·········· Weekly ··········· Monthly ··········· Yearly

Time allotted to spend for this activity:

What what ways will this activity support your mental well-being?

Create a value statement for what you are looking to gain by participating in this activity?

66

99

Practice Yoga or Stretching Exercises

Doing yoga or stretching exercises can help you feel less stiff and move more easily. Your body reacts to your thoughts and feelings, and activities like stretching can make you more aware of this. You don't have to spend a long time on these exercises —they can be short and simple. You can even do them throughout the day to help your body release emotions and feel better.

Frequency you look to participate in this activity:

Daily ·········· Weekly ············ Monthly ············ Yearly

Time allotted to spend for this activity:

What what ways will this activity support your mental well-being?

_____

_____

Create a value statement for what you are looking to gain by participating in this activity?

66 _____

99

Remember: Movement Is Medicine

Exercise isn't punishment for what you ate or how you look. It's a celebration of what your body can do. It's medicine for your mind, a boost for your mood, and fuel for your dreams.

Every step counts. Every stretch matters. Every movement makes a difference. You don't have to be perfect—you just have to begin.
Your body wants to move. Your brain needs the boost. Your emotions crave the release. Give yourself the gift of Vitamin E through exercise. Start today, start small, but most importantly, just start.

The strongest, happiest, most confident version of yourself is waiting. All it takes is moving your body to set that person free. You've got this!

SELF CARE VITAMIN E

Defeciency Assessment

Instructions: For each statement, check the number that best describes how often this is true for you.

Rating Scale:

1 = Never/Rarely 2 = Sometimes 3 = Often 4 = Always/Almost Always

---

PART 1: Physical Activity Level	1	2	3	4
1. I engage in physical activity that makes me breathe harder.				
2. I move my body in some way every day.				
3. I take stairs instead of elevators when possible.				
4. I enjoy the physical activities I choose to do.				
5. Exercise is a regular part of my weekly routine.				

Part 1   Score: ___/20

PART 2: Energy & Strength	1	2	3	4
6. I have enough energy for my daily activities.				
7. I can carry groceries or books without feeling weak.				
8. My body feels strong and capable.				
9. I bounce back quickly after physical activity.				
10. I have good endurance for activities I enjoy.				

Part 2   Score: ___/20

PART 3: Movement & Flexibility	1	2	3	4
11. I stretch or move to relieve stiffness.				
12. My body moves freely without major pain or restriction.				
13. I take movement breaks during long sitting periods.				
14. I notice and respond when my body feels tight.				
15. Daily tasks like bending or reaching are easy for me.				

Part 3   Score: ___/20

PART 4: Mental & Emotional Benefits	1	2	3	4
16. Physical activity improves my mood.				
17. I use movement to manage stress.				
18. Exercise helps me think more clearly.				
19. I feel confident after being active.				
20. Movement helps me sleep better.				

Part 4   Score: ___/20

PART 5: Consistency & Enjoyment	1	2	3	4
21. I look forward to being active.				
22. I find ways to make exercise fun.				
23. Bad weather doesn't stop me from moving my body.				
24. I try new physical activities to stay interested.				
25. Being active feels like self-care, not punishment.				

Part 5   Score: ___/20

Calculate Your Total Vitamin E Level:

Add all five part scores: _____/100

Understanding Your Results:

Total Score 80-100: Highly Active - Vitamin E Strong!

You've made movement a natural part of life! Your body and mind are reaping the benefits. You understand that exercise is self-care, not punishment. Keep inspiring others!

Your focus: Maintain variety and help others discover joyful movement.

Total Score 60-79: Moderately Active - Vitamin E Good

You're doing well with regular movement but have room to grow. You see the benefits but might struggle with consistency. You're on the right path!

Your focus: Build consistency and find more activities you truly enjoy.

Total Score 40-59: Somewhat Active - Vitamin E Needs Boost

You move sometimes but not enough to feel the full benefits. Exercise might feel like a chore rather than self-care. Time to find your movement joy!

Your focus: Start small with activities that feel fun, not forced.

Total Score Under 40: Inactive - Vitamin E Deficiency

Movement is largely missing from your life. This affects your energy, mood, and health. Don't worry—every body can become more active!

Your focus: Begin with 5-minute gentle movements and build slowly.

Physical Warning Signs (Check all that apply):

☐ I get winded climbing one flight of stairs

☐ My back/neck hurts from sitting too long

☐ I feel stiff and creaky when I wake up

☐ Simple tasks like carrying laundry feel hard

☐ I have trouble sleeping even when tired

☐ My energy crashes every afternoon

☐ I feel physically older than my age

☐ Standing for long periods is uncomfortable

☐ I avoid activities because I'll be too tired

☐ My mood is consistently low or anxious

If you checked 5 or more: Your body is crying out for movement!

Your Lowest Section Score:

Target your weakest area:

Lowest: Physical Activity Level? → Try: Daily walks, dancing to music, active video games

Lowest: Energy & Strength? → Try: Bodyweight exercises, carrying groceries differently, stair climbing

Lowest: Movement & Flexibility? → Try: Morning stretches, yoga videos, movement breaks

Lowest: Mental & Emotional Benefits? → Try: Exercise for mood not appearance, moving meditation, nature walks

Lowest: Consistency & Enjoyment? → Try: Exercise buddy, trying new activities, reward system

Your Movement Prescription:

Based on your score, here's your activity plan:

Score 80-100: Maintain 30+ minutes daily + try new challenges monthly

Score 60-79: 20-30 minutes daily + find two activities you love

Score 40-59: 15 minutes daily + focus on enjoyment over intensity

Score Under 40: 5-10 minutes daily + celebrate every movement

Movement Menu:

Choose activities based on your style:

For the Busy Person:

☐ Park farther away   ☐ Desk exercises

☐ Walking meetings   ☐ Dance while cooking

☐ Commercial break movements

For the Social Butterfly:

☐ Walking with friends   ☐ Dance classes

☐ Team sports   ☐ Group fitness

☐ Active volunteering

For the Solo Mover:

☐ YouTube workouts   ☐ Nature walks

☐ Swimming   ☐ Home yoga

☐ Running/jogging

For the Fun Seeker:

☐ Trampoline parks   ☐ Hula hooping

☐ Roller skating   ☐ Dancing games

☐ Playground workouts

For the Gentle Mover:

☐ Chair exercises   ☐ Tai chi

☐ Water aerobics   ☐ Gentle stretching

☐ Slow walks

Your Weekly Movement Plan:

Fill in realistic activities for each day:

Monday: _____   Tuesday: _____   Wednesday: _____

Thursday: _____   Friday: _____   Saturday: _____

Sunday: _____

Total weekly minutes goal: _____

Barrier Busters:

Match your excuse to a solution:

"I don't have time" → 5-minute movement breaks, exercise while watching TV

"I'm too tired" → Gentle movement creates energy, start with 2 minutes

"It's boring" → Music, podcasts, exercise buddy, new activities

"I'm too out of shape" → Everyone starts somewhere, modify everything

"It hurts" → Start gentler, check form, see doctor if needed

"Bad weather" → Indoor videos, mall walking, stair climbing

Movement Mood Tracker:

Track how movement affects your mood:

Before exercise mood (1-10): ___ After exercise mood (1-10): ___ Energy before (1-10): ___ Energy after (1-10): ___ Sleep quality that night (1-10): ___

Pattern I notice:

My Exercise Support System:

Movement buddy: _

Backup indoor activity: _

Favorite playlist: _

Best time of day for me: _

Reward for consistency: _

Small Steps Success List:

Celebrate EVERY movement:

☐ Took the stairs once

☐ Danced to one song

☐ Stretched for 2 minutes

☐ Walked to mailbox

☐ Did 5 squats

☐ Played with pet actively

☐ Cleaned vigorously

☐ Carried groceries mindfully

☐ Stood instead of sat

☐ Parked farther away

My Movement Commitment:

Movement that sounds most fun:

Smallest step I can take today:

Time I'll protect for movement:

How I'll track my progress:

What I'll tell myself when I don't want to move:

Body Appreciation List:

Write 5 things your body does for you:

1.
2.
3.
4.
5.

Remember to thank your body with movement!

Remember: Exercise isn't about earning food or punishing yourself. It's about celebrating what your body can do and feeling good in your own skin. Every movement counts, no matter how small. Your body wants to move—listen to it!

My Vitamin E Goal for This Week:

Quick Movement Reset:

When you need instant energy:

1. Stand up and stretch tall
2. Do 10 jumping jacks (or arm circles)
3. Take 5 deep breaths
4. Shake out your whole body
5. Smile—you just moved!

Your strongest, most energetic self is just a movement away. Start now!

Your Wellness, Your Way

Create your personalized
self-care plan

7 Creating Your Personalized Self-Care Plan

Everything you do in life—from school and work to hanging out with friends—gets easier when you feel good physically and mentally. Imagine starting your day knowing exactly how to handle whatever stress comes your way. Having a plan makes all the difference. Without one, stress can feel like a huge wave crashing over you.

Throughout this book, you've learned about five Self-Care Vitamins that work like supplements for your mind and emotions. Each vitamin helps in its own special way:

- Vitamin A for Awareness helps you understand yourself
- Vitamin B for Balance keeps your life organized
- Vitamin C for Connection strengthens relationships
- Vitamin D for Detox clears out negativity
- Vitamin E for Exercise boosts your energy and mood

Now comes the exciting part: creating YOUR personal wellness plan. Just like mixing ingredients to make your favorite smoothie, you'll combine different self-care activities to create a routine that fits your life perfectly.

This chapter will show you how to build a plan that helps you feel strong, focused, and ready for anything life brings your way.

Checking Your Current Self-Care Levels

Before creating your plan, let's see where you stand with each vitamin. Think of this as a wellness check-up for your mind and emotions.

Vitamin A: Awareness Check

Self-awareness is like having good eyesight for your inner world. It helps you see your thoughts and feelings clearly. When your Vitamin A levels are strong, you understand yourself better and make smarter choices.

Try these quick assessments:
- Daily Reflection: Write for 5 minutes about your day. What patterns do you notice in your thoughts and feelings?
- Mood Moments: Set three phone alarms. When they ring, quickly note how you're feeling. Are you stressed? Happy? Focused?
- Friend Feedback: Ask someone close to you: "What mood do I seem to be in most often?" Their answer might surprise you.

Vitamin B: Balance Check

Balance keeps your life running smoothly, like a well-oiled machine. Too much work and no play makes you tired. Too much play and no work causes stress. Finding the sweet spot is key.

Check your balance with these tools:

- Time Tracker: For one day, write down how you spend each hour. How much goes to work/school? Fun? Rest? Self-care?
- Energy Map: Rate your energy (1-10) every few hours for a week. When are you most energetic? Most tired?
- Yes/No List: Keep track of what you agree to do. Are you saying yes to too much? Practice saying "Let me think about it."

Vitamin C: Connection Check

Connections are like sunshine for your soul. Good relationships make everything in life feel easier and more fun. But not all interactions feed your spirit—some drain it.

Evaluate your connections:

- People Power: List your top 5 people. After spending time with each, do you feel energized or exhausted?
- Sharing Scale: How often do you share real feelings (not just "I'm fine")? Daily? Weekly? Never?
- Support Squad: Who would you call with good news? Bad news? If the list is short, it's time to build stronger connections.

Vitamin D: Detox Check

Just like cleaning your room makes it nicer to live in, detoxing your mind makes life more peaceful. Mental clutter—from toxic people to to negative thoughts—weighs you down.

Assess your detox needs:
- Screen Time Reality: Track your daily phone/computer time. Is it helping or hurting your mood?
- Space Check: Look around your room. Does the clutter stress you out? A messy space often equals a messy mind.
- Thought Patrol: For one day, notice negative thoughts. How many times do you think "I can't" or "I'm not good enough"?

Vitamin E: Exercise Check

Movement is medicine for your body and mind. It doesn't have to mean running marathons—any movement counts. The key is finding what you enjoy.

Measure your movement:
- Activity Log: Write down all physical activity for a week. Include everything from walking to class to playing sports.
- Body Signals: Notice how your body feels. Stiff? Tired? Energetic? Your body tells you what it needs.
- Fun Factor: List physical activities you actually enjoy. If the list is empty, it's time to experiment!

Building Your Successful Self-Care Plan

Now that you know where you stand, let's build a plan that actually works for your life.

Make It Personal

Your plan should fit YOU, not what others think you should do. Love quiet time alone? Don't force yourself into group activities. Hate meditation? Try dancing instead.

Ask yourself:
- What makes me feel recharged?
- When do I have free time?
- What activities fit my personality?

Start Small, Think Big

Rome wasn't built in a day, and neither is a good self-care routine. Starting with too much leads to quitting.

Week 1: Add ONE 5-minute activity Week 2: Extend to 10 minutes or add another 5-minute activity Week 3: Keep building slowly

Small wins lead to big changes!

Find Your "Why"

Write down WHY self-care matters to you. Maybe:

- "I want energy to enjoy time with friends"
- "I want to feel less stressed about tests"
- "I want to be happier"

Put this somewhere you'll see it daily. When motivation drops (it will), your "why" brings you back.

Create Accountability

Making changes alone is tough. Set yourself up for success:

- Tell a friend about your plan
- Use phone reminders
- Track progress in a journal
- Reward yourself for sticking to it

Your Personal Wellness Recipe

Time to put it all together! Fill in your plan:

My Vitamin A (Awareness)

Activity: __ When I'll do it: __ For how long: __

My Vitamin B (Balance)

Activity: __ When I'll do it: __ For how long: __

My Vitamin C (Connection)

Activity: __ When I'll do it: __ For how long: __

My Vitamin D (Detox)

Activity: __ When I'll do it: __ For how long: __

My Vitamin E (Exercise)

Activity: __ When I'll do it: __ For how long: __

The Busy Student Plan (15 minutes daily):

- Morning: 3-minute breathing (Vitamin A)
- Lunch: 5-minute walk (Vitamin E)
- Evening: 5-minute text check-in with friend (Vitamin C)
- Before bed: 2-minute gratitude list (Vitamin D)

The Weekend Warrior Plan (for those with more weekend time):

- Weekdays: 5-minute morning stretch
- Saturdays: 1-hour activity with friends
- Sundays: 30-minute room clean and journal session

The Night Owl Plan (for evening people):

- After dinner: 10-minute walk
- Before homework: 5-minute dance break
- Before bed: 10-minute journal and stretch

Troubleshooting Common Problems:

"I keep forgetting!"

- Set phone alarms
- Link activities to habits you already have
- Put reminders where you'll see them

"I don't have time!"

- Start with 2-minute activities
- Combine activities (walk with a friend = Vitamin C + E)
- Replace scrolling time with self-care time

"Nothing seems to work!"

- Try each activity for at least a week
- Adjust timing or intensity
- Remember: progress isn't always obvious at first

Your Self-Care Promise

Write and sign your commitment:

"I promise to take care of myself because I deserve to feel good. I will start small, be patient with myself, and celebrate every success. When I skip a day (it happens), I'll simply start again tomorrow. My well-being matters."
Signed: __ Date: __

The Power of Your Plan

Creating your self-care plan is like giving yourself a superpower. When stress hits, you know exactly what to do. When emotions overwhelm you, you have tools ready. When life gets crazy, your plan keeps you grounded.

This isn't about being perfect. It's about being prepared. Some days you'll nail every activity. Other days you'll manage just one. Both are victories.

Your plan will grow and change as you do. What works today might need tweaking next month. That's not failure—that's growth. The important thing is starting and keeping going, even imperfectly.

Remember: You can't pour from an empty cup. Taking care of yourself isn't selfish—it's necessary. When you feel good, everyone around you benefits. Your best self is waiting, and your personalized self-care plan is the map to get there.

Start today. Start small. But definitely start. Future you will be so grateful you did.

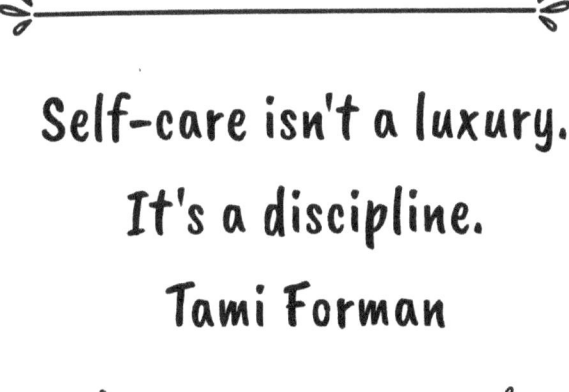

Self-care isn't a luxury.
It's a discipline.
Tami Forman

Design Life Hub Resources

Intentional.U App

Apple Store

Google Play Store

LEARN MORE

DLH Newsletter

Resources

Stay Connected

Facebook

Instagram

THANK YOU

Thank you for your purchase! If you have enjoyed this purchase please consider dropping us a review. It takes 5 seconds and helps a small business like ours.